T0171038

NIGHT BURIAL

THE COLORADO PRIZE FOR POETRY

NIGHT BURIAL

poems

KATE BOLTON BONNICI

The Center for Literary Publishing
Colorado State University

For information about permission to reproduce
selections from this book, write to
The Center for Literary Publishing
attn: Permissions
9105 Campus Delivery
Colorado State University
Fort Collins, Colorado 80523-9105.

Printed in the United States of America.

Library of Congress Cataloging-in-Publication Data

Names: Bonnici, Kate Bolton, 1979- author.
Title: Night burial : poems / Kate Bolton Bonnici.
Description: Fort Collins, Colorado : The Center for Literary Publishing,
    Colorado State University, [2020]
Identifiers: LCCN 2020035623 (print) | LCCN 2020035624 (ebook) |
    ISBN 9781885635730 (paperback) | ISBN 9781885635747 (ebook)
Subjects: LCSH: Mothers and daughters--Poetry. | Grief--Poetry. |
    LCGFT: Poetry.
Classification: LCC PS3602.O657426 N54 2020 (print) | LCC PS3602.O657426
    (ebook) | DDC 811/.6--dc23
LC record available at https://lccn.loc.gov/2020035623
LC ebook record available at https://lccn.loc.gov/2020035624

The paper used in this book meets the minimum requirements of the
American National Standard for Information Sciences-Permanence of Paper
for Printed Library Materials, ANSI Z39.48-1984.

for my mother, 1946–2017

Then there is this other
abyss that opens up between
the body and what had been
its inside. . . .

—Julia Kristeva, "Stabat Mater"

CONTENTS

III. NIGHT BURIAL

IV. THE FORMER OBJECT OF MY EVERYTHING

I. FALL RISK

Mine eyes dry & cannot see have
mercy my heart weak & cannot feel have
mercy our words smoke & cannot touch have
mercy

on the woods they are burning
on the storm it moves over the fields
on the schoolhouse it trembles
on the fruits of your labors
one of which is her
we cry

"CORPSES LIKE NIGHT SOIL / GET CARTED OFF"

[Heraclitus]

This is not a tragedy / it does not satisfy
the unities of action / or time or place Aristotle
would say this is / incomplete in the whole
& on the whole / I would agree this is
not your tragedy this is / a scrap a slip a fragment
a swatch of fabric cut / off the roll laid against
the old pillow to see how / it becomes your coloring
or the shades of the room / window shades down
other shades hovering / this is a snippet a snag
a snapshot Barthes's / *what has been* & is
no more this does / not satisfy a poetics
it's too ordinary not the / ordinary of comfort food
the ordinary of sand / in your teeth each
grain of dead quartz / helical when a hurricane
hits after midnight / & it's no longer the day
it was but has become / another morning mourning
we are carried through / the gulf sand clings
disrupts what could be said / of location & when
the question / *Is this pretend?*
compose decompose / recompose
one day the red chair / one day the garden one day
only the lilies still bloom / they are made of silk

IT WAS A COMMON NIGHT

1.

Other versions thus begun the mother dies
sooner or later, in childbirth or not.
In one she dies of joy. (In the poem, still
alive although ill.)

My mother remembers the echo
from her mother's heels in the hall,
her mother's own cancer endometrial.
My mother wore boots.

When my mother rose, blood
there in the toilet, blood to the brim
it seemed or seems through
my early recollection. I'm four.

A story crux comes with the removal
of children one by one.

2.

My earliest memory of my daughters they
will have forgotten, which is not the same
as not having known.
Our first experience is thirst.

Yesterday I saw exhibits
from *The Exquisite Uterus Project*,
every instrument of the illustrated uteri
artfully cut from my mother's body.

Cross-stitch staples plait her abdomen.
Each closure point aches when she must
lean up to drink. Each drink filling in
that narrowest time

we call
the days to come.

HOUSEHOLD TALES

I do not know how the boy's body was recovered,
how he was lifted from the seeds of things, or when.
What kind of grain he fell into
my grandmother does not remember.
Psyche could not separate the seeds without help. I assemble a bed.
If the upper bunk breaks both the assemblage and the decision
to let a daughter sleep there are mine.
It was my mother's cousin's son who drowned in a grain bin.
We had a farm and horses. I would reach my hand into the oats
until I disappeared. Rats big as a forearm.
We say the boy "drowned."
If water signifies a travel narrative, then before reaching
the black fountain, Psyche was charged with separating a mass of seeds.
All for wanting Love to come back again.

MORROW, MORROW, VALENTINE

They say hope survives because we lack
foresight yet here

I've read the story & know
to miss you before you're gone—

sorrow does not call me love
but will when you are lost

a child who cannot know to mourn
your possibilities, the particular

way you would pronounce
a word like *empty*—

the tale of the swans' sister is a tale
told not at bedtime—take

her babies, mark her mouth, blame
her congealèd heart

her blood a thick Valentine
of love & consumption—

I've read the story
& can't pretend

what happens elsewhere
happens to another, to some other,

at some other time
able to quiet the calls at the door.

WITCHSPEAK

Someone asked the meaning
     of *Dr. Faustus*
     in a secular world. I did not say whose secular world—

In the pamphlet, agèd Agnes is called *witch*
     for praying her *pater noster* (hard to undo
     the body's learning)

In her hands, beads. In her hands, a hallowed practice. In her foolish hands.

Teat, the prong of udder where milk moves
Teat, the word once used for blood pact
Teat, a conviction

Teat sounds far from *tear* or *tear* but all
     will open a passage

of liquids.
     The concern those years remembered in nights
     I nursed children—milk seeps and the question of enough

Since someone is always thirsty,
I deliver a child daily into want

BURN PERMIT

In no case will the person requesting the permit allow the
fire to be unattended until it is dead out.
—Alabama Code § 9-13-11(c)(1)(c), Department of Forestry

1.

A story: go to hell,
pluck three hairs from the devil's head,
a head I picture part bald anyway only
I must reorient now that my mother's hair went.

Waiting with her in the infusion center
I read *The Winter's Tale,* the one where
Mama comes back.

That she is living,
Were it but told you, should be hooted at
Like an old tale: but it appears she lives.

2.

Forestry
will consider many variables
of condition, why
my father says, you can't burn the longleafs.

Smoke management requires you
to wait for a North wind,
but you won't get a North wind
when you need it.

Smoke will follow a hollow like water
fills a vessel to level.

3.

Not the first time but an early time
leaving home I went to Rouen, France.
Joan of Arc burned there in 1431.
Before I knew this, I dressed as a crusader,
recited Shaw's version of her.

We named our first daughter her name but not
for fire, I think for something other.
My mother's name.
Sainte Jeanne, priez pour nous.

4.

May 1st marks Forestry's burn ban,
52 days after Mama's cancer scan

Lite-Brite lit cells,
lil' Rice Krispies, only quiet

intraperitoneal chemo
fills up the cavity cup—

cisplatin / paclitaxel—
cycle now Day 1 / Day 8 / week's rest

the longleafs will outlive her—
and grow a holy forest

BURNT OFFERING

Old stories say burn the skin
of what you've become

to bring back before's self
or burn the born-in skin

to keep you new
or burn the wolf pines

but not the burrows
where the animals wait for light.

FALL RISK

In 1615 after leaving Lemnos, George Sandys translated Homer to describe
the island of *the fabulous fall of Vulcan,* the one *who signifieth fire.*

All day I was in falling; and at night
On Lemnos fell: life had forsooke me quite.

The ancients, Sandys wrote, *used sundry ceremonies: ceremony which giveth*
repute unto things in themselves but trivial.

Mine own: wake when it's dark out but dark just passed over to morning.
Make coffee. Doze. Having fallen, the house does not yet arise.

All day I was in falling; and at night. Depleted after chemotherapy
my mother is labeled *fall risk.*

The earth where Vulcan landed received *those excellent virtues*
of curing of wounds, stopping of fluxes, expulsing poisons, &c.

All day landlocked, chemo seasick, the body unsealed by a poisonous cure.
Cure: mystery's translation of care and preserve, the word we offer shyly

and with a small falling forward.

I keep cushions on the floor so my younger one will land softly.
Such are the shrines of the household gods.

COMING, MAMA, TO CARRY

I imagine the call,
the moan through breath
that wants words to open,
not for the song to lie down

RECURRENCE

Happy birthday, daughter. Tomorrow we'll dance with bubble wands at the park

Tomorrow my father will drive my mother for a paracentesis

to remove malignant fluid from her abdomen

Yesterday your father looked so young, I said *like a kid*

You said *like someone who still has a mother*

Walking the path of
what got you here I can only
wonder at the

X chromosomes that plotted you on this
x-axis where I wish, like the azaleas, your
xylem cells could pull up water

THE PALACE

1.

Opening the guidebook to see
how Henry VIII took castles
& chocolate, my child finds fire.
Reading—the danger—
Easter Day, 1986.
Perished. I search out
rose gardens, cold food storage,
a queen's bedchamber,
but she wants none of it.
How did you get out of the maze? she asks.
Her fingers are hard—this
is the thing of her—pressing,
each time, to the blaze.

2.

A painting stranger than Ovid's undressed lovers lounging upside down
on walls I remember. Henry, Edward, Mary, Elizabeth. How they stood.
Together, stilled, each caught closing in on the other.

How did you get out of the maze?

3.

My hope is the tight coil
of her own six years
preceded by naught

will let me make these
nineteen eighties the baroque
fire of another time.
Did you reach the center? she asks.
A center is preceded by
every blessed thing.

4.

Mother, she says, a try-on word turning her hard to something far.
She opens to fire once more.

"IN THE OLD TIME, THEY USED TO PUTT A PENNY IN THE DEAD PERSONS MOUTH"

[John Aubrey, c. 1688]

Through a crowded mall
you held my hand
we believed our luck
tossed that penny in the fountain.

THE CHILD BREAKS A GLASS OF MILK

Mama, carry me to the table—
      where I should have been before

when the glass fell
      we both felt

give out

then I breathed in the fat
      of her cheek

and—

II. ORDINARY TIME

"IN YOUR ABSENCE THERE ARE NO MORTAL BANQUETS."

[*Homeric Hymns,* "To Hestia"]

1.

Too late, the one you love cannot be
        located
Too late, how to summon—
        Too late how to say

2.

My father says it plainly
        Jean. You.
Each flows down a silk-
        leafed grave

inside of which is the body
        I was inside of
when only becoming
        a body

& I know *flows*
        is the wrong word—
can't capture what passes
        & what remains

3.

What remains
        remains to be seen
never
        is what I'm afraid of

4.

Fear, what didn't come
          those nights watching
you or should I say it wasn't what fear
          I'd expected

waking up midnight
          to coyotes
howling a moon circle
          around the room

while you slept
          (so we slept)
I didn't see the small terrier
          (always patient as you vomited)

& knew I'd forgotten him
          This was his song
of terror
          & his sacrifice

5.

But he'd made no offering   he was there
          beneath the bed
there where I wanted to go   there
          where time
also hides

6.

Document times
          & amounts
measure of pain volume of vomit
          & when   (numbers matter)

meds get harder when you are
          N.P.O. (nothing by mouth)
I learned abbreviated Latin listening
          to you dictate charts

years before electronic records
          years before this
years you called the hospital from the den
          you said
thum & cleared your throat beginning
          each sentence

I sat beside you, half reading & a child
          remembers the morning
of her mother's
          voice

7.

That diagnosis is a death sentence, you said
          Yours is
It was
          It will be

8.

I have not seen the ghost
       of my mother
become blue like a bottle in the smoke
       & broken

blue the color of her shirt the day of
       & the day before
she died with blue
       mottling

her feet her ankles her legs meaning
       tissue becoming
dead the line of blue
       under each vein

in her hands held
       warm under ours
warming a body no longer
       warming itself

9.

Before, we drank hot percolator coffee
       in thin-lipped cups
at the table where you
       were a daughter too

10.

As daughter you remain
        insoluble
the second- & third-
        person object of our longing

You are you & the mother
        I speak to
or speak of
        & will that become increasingly so

now that each day is memorial
        each ends with here lies
buried here lies bones joints
        & cataracts undoing

undone a past tense
        I can't reckon with
Let us resist the history
        of every word between us

11.

Between us every word
        is dirt-swaddled   just-born
Below the one-ton cemetery mower
        a wildflower seed mix

12.

Mix Miralax into Coca-Cola
        hoping to keep your gut alive
what it comes down to is
        you want a cold Coke

False equation—
        a sip equals stronger
equals more chemo equals
        alive & if I could go back

to your last almost-dawn
        asking to sleep on the sofa
by the Christmas tree
        I would say yes

13.

This reminds me, you said at 3 AM
        wiping your wet gown, *of*
Hasten, Jason, bring the basin—
        Too late, bring the mop!

MEASURE OF ORDINARY TIME

Like a dead animal, she said, *the eyelashes too.*

My older daughter notices.
Beanie, you have no lashes.

My mother is giving my daughters
the piano she's had since age 12.

I don't need it.
They do.

When you get the new piano,
their sheet music won't fall.

She wanted to know the songs
would hold.

FOR MY MOTHER WHOSE MOTHER IS ILL

You go to church when she's sick,
pray for or to or with something

caught, slightest glass
in the pad of your foot after

breaking the jelly jar we drank from,
only it's her foot, the tissue

of which has gone paper dead,
and in prayer you kneel to listen

or only hear without listening,
and you know with your hands

on the wooden back of a pew
that the body is the smallest offering

and your only one. You want a chorus
of *this then this* to sing in you,

but it's never that easy
when you aren't alone.

This week my mother's mother fell. Hemorrhagic stroke.
First night home from the ICU my mother
dropped her mother trying to transfer her from the toilet.

"LET THE QUICK THEN CAST FORTH THE DEAD"

[Jane Sharp, *The Midwives Book,* 1671]

Passing a uterine blood
clot on the shotgun
side of the truck
felt like what it would feel
like to lay an egg
in a chicken hauler.
The dirt road
a practiced
hand beneath us,
holding mudslides,
erasure, the palm-
up question why.
It'll hold it all,
and so what—

BLOOD LINES

Daughter, I lie with you on the crackling chuck pad, burning where your body

opened mine to be born, the sacred stitched up and pink

in lines I once caused upon my mother.

For days after she shuffled close-legged, rent perineum, her rewritten body a shaky

glass egg that could lope away end-over-end down any street.

"SHE DIED — *THIS* WAS THE WAY SHE DIED."

[Emily Dickinson]

Dad held her after she'd yanked out the NG tube and
we understood then that when
she went home it would be her
last time. Nurses caught their breath
watching the end of the doctor who was
one of them, done

for and done
in by the same ovaries they had and
wheeled out by a son they'd seen born who was
himself going gray. Only—when
the doc got to the waiting car, she took a breath,
fixed her

smile, said to her
husband, Let's take a drive, I'm not ready to be done.
He held his breath,
didn't ask, What do you mean by that? and
started driving. When
is my next chemo? was

the question that did him in, was
what made him sure we'd misread her
body, put her on a course to dying when
she wasn't—what have we done?—
she wasn't dead and
here she was beside him, a breath

in, a barely-breath
out, and he could barely breathe. It was
hard to remember the three miles home and

odd to use the blinker with her
next to him alive and not undone.
He wanted hope. She wanted ice cream. When

they got home she walked in on her own. When
she walked in she vomited until she couldn't breathe
and when she was done,
mouth green-wet, she said she was
calling her
oncologist to schedule chemo and

that she wasn't done when
she left the hospital and she couldn't be done while any breath
was inside her
still.

PRIMER

After lightning count the seconds
before thunder. Seconds equal miles & the rain
continues. Sunshiny like the
devil's beating his wife with a frying pan.
Everywhere that yellow
fungal
glow marking how you're gone from
here. We hold our hands high as if asking for
incarnation or the impossible (not the same).
Just keep breathing, we said. Just keep the heart beating. Just
keep some soul stuff or the molecular compounds of
love alive in the room, in you, in
me, but of course
no, not happening. We counted breaths
out, counted heartbeats, measured blood
pressure. All lower lower lower like seconds
quicker after the sound of thunder & the
rain coming harder.
Sun that's gone, storm that's closer.
Thunder-lightning almost one on top of the other. We're
under a band shown purple by the radar
visionaries. Only we aren't watching the rain
winding like winding sheets, like knots of tumor on the
X-ray or the nuclear scans
you had back when we thought this storm was at its
zenith, but you cannot know a zenith until an end.

III. NIGHT BURIAL

Quiet & you are not among the
quick but the dead I
quickened once in your womb you who felt my own
quickening

rested your hand on my
round belly at 20 weeks
riding to Pensacola a daughter
reached

stretched pressed her hand
slight against my
skin to your swan-soft hand

toward you we keep reaching for what we cannot
touch we keep
trying to send signals in
texts, tulips, rocks stacked day by day along the walkway

Look upon your servant
looking homeward
lying without life while we
lift up our love as formless offering

Thanksgiving I sat with her
in the sun, sky blue as a church fan
imprinted with the rapture

neither of us delirious
in the cumulative

She was smiling

fled to the woods   found a hollow tree   one could pick roots
by light of morning   climbed in the tree   small sustaining things

My other grandmother has stopped sewing.
Does this make her no longer
who she was?

I gave her a porcelain thimble from the airport store,
now breakable & impractical the object
meant to give her one last force.

After the rains a path of needles,
after the winds a path of pins.

Just wear it
Mama
We're washing the rest

She wears a blue fishing shirt
not soft enough
all we had without vomit

My last picture
taken the morning
before

How to know someone is dying? Check their feet for mottling.
We covered yours/hers—when? Before or after?
Before is short. But, the after—

In the opera, Manon speaks
to sing the soul's leaving,
chant I can just hear
above all that's inland
of the interior.

Keen & cry out for the
kingdom what was
knitted frays &
keeps no terrible watch

My husband holds my hand
a day after his birthday which would be
his mother's birthday were she here
for her birthday.

My mother fell into a sleep
that for hours was a bad sleep
until it was no longer sleep

For one minute
I left the room

& my mother
stopped breathing forever

For one minute
I left the room

& what does it mean

Now I breathe this forever in

She left the room & she stopped breathing

I left the room & you stopped breathing

You left the room & I stopped breathing

Enter Mary
enter Holy Spirit I say
enter Holy Ghost
enter & be merciful
any ghost at all

Daughters sing from the backseat
of snowstorms, their paper voices
interwoven, one an inch behind.
Thus they sing the sound
of their own yet-unmeasured selves.

On foot my daughters aim stiff-arms, a *Stop!*
to cars in the crosswalk. *Careful,*
Mama. These drivers
will flat run you down.

Give me haint blue inside of which
to not let you
& I will choose the other
not the color to keep your ghost

outside but inside
outside on the porch it is too cold
colder than you remember

your arms blue under blue sleeves
blue veins what I could see
we must keep the warm in
keep you here
how you might still be

When she came home
from the hospital
my daughters painted
my mother's nails
turquoise.

Did we leave the polish on—

I am mad at you
being dead

being dead
who can I be mad
at & where

why couldn't you stay
in the maze?

You, she, we, I can't,
it's gone, feel it

Night burial, a winter sky, a winter ground
not quite frozen, not quite Christmas

quiet, we left together, leaving you
to become what you will become

what we will become without you with us
we left you at the edge of town in your new dead town

the priest said you must be
in the ground before dark

it was dark out when you stopped breathing
but when we laid you to rest not quite, not quite dark, starlit—

You lie here do
you like it here do
you love here
you are loved here

here
I brought you
zinnias

An ancient loop—someone
looking means someone's gone.
Something unequal
makes its way forward.

Your mother dies.
The most ordinary thing.

IV. THE FORMER OBJECT OF MY EVERYTHING

"FOR THIS DAIE YOUR DAUGHTER HATHE BENE BOTHE ALIVE AND DEADE"

[Euripides]

Not alive then dead, alive & dead
which is how it happens, I saw it

Each time we say *this* it is a *now* that has passed
& so never is
or can we say never ceases

For this day
& this day
& this

To my grandmother, my mother is a daughter
I have daughters, one
grandmother, no living mother

The messenger tries to stop time, which doesn't flow
it gets caught, not a driving force, an eddy

The messenger tries to capture it
but what the messenger shows is

time's interruption
isn't needed to see you
alive & dead

both you have been & you are
on this day

TRANSCENDENTAL ÉTUDE

A Mylar star
balloon almost to the sun,
backlit, bulging blue, something
lost or borrowed, let
go, ghosted, hands reaching
from the ground, reaching
that can't be explained
or bettered, as in, I can't,
no way, it's gone,
a freed form
on the move, or some short,
shiny wish.

GALLERY

after the Blue Boy *restoration project at the Huntington Library*

inside the portrait gallery
inside
I've come looking
for your soul
& we're close

everyone is dead
I've come to see skeletons
of a blue boy not your own
your own bones clacking
like on the day of return

your bones
soft smudges
or not
once
once
over the blue boy

what are the details
we can see
long dead & of what
what does it mean
to cure

the look of death
in your preservation
the conservator keeps a semblance alive
tried to keep you alive
(blood inside blue) only
the boy

living I dare not say
in your present you had
to let the sun lengthen
but taking your glasses off
you hear what comes

& where immortal only
in a vision of how
blue behind pines
could feel cold
from the bones

PRIMER

Annunciation: address your mother where she lies
below Bahiagrass. She's not
calling out a response cause she's
dead.

Death you know now is not a triumphal and
emblazoned entry into elsewhere. *Keep
fighting!* signs fucking stupid when you're dead. Better
Gone fishing or *Gone shopping* or *GTFO*.
Here lies, the one you choose
instead. Announcing

in present tense
just a location's locus of dislocation.
(Keep to the plot,
lower her into a plot, this
merry little plot festooned with
nonce arrangements
ordered seasonally.

Or, better, remember how we
performed the platitudes of
quite (im)possible
recovery not

realizing the real chances were so
slim, a sliver of slim, like the plotted point at which a
tangent touches a circle.

That slim.)
Upside of twelve months turns *Fight on!* to *In memory of,*

vestal painted
wings elevate name, host, virgin before Gabriel rings in
Xmas. I curse your culmination, curse this undead
year rotating its bedazzled and fleshy
zodiac, curse all the flash of these dumb stars.

TO LAY SOD ON A GRAVE

Begin with a body, but let the body stop breathing
Let your own body stop breathing
Until you cannot not breathe because
Having begun, your body conspires to continue

Begin by calling the mortuary, but not at once
Do not leave her alone, not even once
Hold her hands, keep them warm, touch her face
With your own warm hands until the undertakers

Come to take her & then you
Begin again with a body lost to you
& here the ground that won't take you
Both. Not now, this ground broken for one

Not yet broken further.

THE FORMER OBJECT OF MY EVERYTHING

When

too

do you offer the absence
that remains your only

remains

The epigraph to this collection comes from Julia Kristeva's essay "Stabat Mater," first published as "Hérethique de l'amour" in *Tel Quel*, 74 (Winter 1977) and republished in *The Kristeva Reader*, edited by Toril Moi, Columbia University Press, 1986.

The title "Corpses like night soil / get carted off," with punctuation silently omitted, is from Heraclitus's Fragment 85, *Fragments: The Collected Wisdom of Heraclitus*, translated by Brooks Haxton, Viking, 2001. Roland Barthes's "what has been" comes from his *Camera Lucida: Reflections on Photography*, translated by Richard Howard, Farrar, Straus and Giroux, 1981.

The title "It Was a Common Night" comes from Emily Dickinson's poem, the first line of which is "The last Night that She lived" and which is numbered 1100 in *The Poems of Emily Dickinson*, edited by R. W. Franklin, Harvard University Press, 1998. The phrase "that narrowest time" is loosely borrowed from the same poem.

The title "Morrow, Morrow, Valentine" comes from an eighteenth-century English children's song to be sung as part of "Valentining," a begging tradition akin to that occurring on other winter feasts like Halloween. This poem also refers to the fairy tale "The Six Swans," one version of which I read in a book from my mother: *The Original Folk and Fairy Tales of the Brothers Grimm*, translated and edited by Jack Zipes, illustrated by Andrea Dezsö, Princeton University Press, 2014.

"Burn Permit" contains lines from Shakespeare's *The Winter's Tale*, 5.3.115–17, *The Arden Shakespeare Complete Works*, edited by Richard Proudfoot, Ann Thompson, and David Scott Kastan, Bloomsbury, 2014.

"Fall Risk" contains lines from Book I of George Sandys's travel narrative *A Relation of a Journey begun Anno Domini 1610*. London: W. Barren, 1615. EEBO.

The title "In the old time, they used to putt a Penny in the dead persons mouth" is from John Aubrey's *Remaines of Gentilisme and Judaisme* (c. 1688), contained in *Three Prose Works,* edited by John Buchanan-Brown, Southern Illinois University Press, 1972.

The title "In your absence there are no mortal banquets" comes from the "Hymn to Hestia" in Sarah Ruden's translation of the *Homeric Hymns,* Hackett, 2005.

The title "let the quick then cast forth the dead" comes from *The Midwives Book, or the Whole Art of Midwifry Discovered, Directing Childbearing Women How to Behave Themselves in Their Conception, Breeding, Bearing, and Nursing of Children,* by Mrs. Jane Sharp, midwife. London: for Simon Miller, at the Star at the West End of St. Paul's, 1671. EEBO.

The title of the sestina "She died — *this* was the way she died" comes from the first line of Emily Dickinson's poem number 154. The end words of the sestina come from the second line of Dickinson's poem: "And when her breath was done."

The title "For this daie your daughter hathe bene bothe alive and deade" comes from *Iphigenia at Aulis,* Euripides, translated by Lady Jane Lumley as *The Tragedie of Euripides called Iphigeneia translated out of Greake into Englisshe,* c. 1553. The "this" argument is a response to Hegel's *Phenomenology of Spirit.*

The title "Transcendental Étude" is taken from Franz Liszt's twelve compositions for piano.

ACKNOWLEDGMENTS

Grateful acknowledgment is made to the following publications in which earlier versions of these poems have appeared or will appear: "Blood Lines," *The Fertile Source;* "Corpses like night soil / get carted off," *Image;* and "Gallery," *In Libris XI: Bibliophilia,* by Richard Ehrlich.

For Kiki Petrosino, who by some miraculous alignment of the stars chose this book and so gave it a life in the world;

For the caring, patient, visionary staff at the Center for Literary Publishing at Colorado State University: Stephanie G'Schwind, Jess Turner, Luke Eldredge, and Jordan Osborne;

For the wisdom and generosity of Katie Ford, Fred D'Aguiar, Harryette Mullen, and Lowell Gallagher;

For my family, though far as the crow flies, still heart-close and soul-sustaining: Don Bolton, Will Bolton, Jeb Bolton, Bebe Foster, Patricia Foster, David Wilder, and Polly Solomon;

And for my daily and dearest beloveds: Dan, Charlotte, and Annie—

I am thankful a thousand thousand times over.

In memory and celebration of my mother-in-law, Maureen Rose Murphy (1951–2016), and my grandmother, Paula Louise Dean Bolton (1927–2018), *requiescant in pace.*

And to my mother, Jean Suzanne Foster Bolton: you remain our armor of light.

This book is set in Constantia
by The Center for Literary Publishing
at Colorado State University.

Copyediting by Jordan Osborne.
Proofreading by Luke Eldredge.
Book design and typesetting by Stephanie G'Schwind.
Cover design by Jess Turner.
Cover art by Jeremy Segrott.
Printing by Books International.